Timawi Denverite

Y0-BPW-369

COUNTRY MUSIC
A look at the men who've made it

Quotations from interviews by
MARINA NICKERSON

Photographs by
CYNTHIA FARAH

Text copyright© 1981 by Marina Nickerson
Photographs copyright© 1981 by Cynthia Farah

All rights reserved in all countries. No part of this book
may be translated or reproduced or used in any form or by
any means whatsoever without the permission of the publisher.

Published by C M Publishing
330 Eubank
El Paso, Texas 79902

Cover art and book design by Michael Steirnagle, El Paso, Texas

Printed in the United States of America by Imperial Litho/Graphics

ISBN 0-9607514-0-8

Library of Congress Cataloging in Publication Data
Farah, Cynthia
Country Music: A Look At The Men Who've Made It.
1. Country musicians-United States-Portraits.
2. Country musicians-United States-Quotations.
I. Nickerson, Marina
II. Title.
ML3524.F37   784.5′2′00922   81-20958
AACR2

Library of Congress Catalog Card Number 81-70858

Introduction

It started with an out-of-the-blue phone call from freelance photographer, Cynthia Farah. She suggested we become a photo/journalist team, concentrating on the country music field. (Since I am the country music critic for *The El Paso Times*, she picked a logical partner.)

Five days later, a fateful meeting occurred at an El Paso radio station where Marty Robbins had gone to do an on-the-air interview with a disc jockey. Unbeknownst to either of us, Cynthia and I both went to the station. I had my tape recorder. She had her camera. That sealed a bond that has led to a wonderful partnership.

Our articles and photos have been published, not only locally, but also in virtually every major country music magazine in the U.S. Since 1979, we have carefully covered the country music scene in El Paso - from honky tonks to nightclubs to auditoriums. Interviews and photo sessions were conducted backstage, on buses and in hotels, restaurants and bars.

This book was the natural result of our endeavors. As a documentary, it is intended to provide an insight into some of the male country music stars. We selected the quotes which we felt best depict their attitudes, describe them and convey their personal and professional opinions. The cross section of men gives an overall view of the diverse backgrounds and personalities of the male artists in the country music field. One thing they all had in common was their cooperation in being interviewed and photographed. Certainly some were more pleasant than others; some more interesting, candid, talkative, etc. Rather than write my impressions, I let their quotes tell the story. And in many cases, the pictures say it all.

The book is not intended to present a composite of all the men in country music. Many "who've made it" are not included; we selected the ones who played the El Paso area.

The songs listed with each artist's name are not their only singles. Nor are they necessarily their biggest hits. We chose songs that were readily associated with the singer and titles that represented the subjects about which these men sing.

We thank each artist - for his contribution to this book and to country music.

And I especially thank Cindy for her creativity, ingeniousness, unfailing sense of humor and relentless motor drive.

Marina Nickerson

All photos were shot on 35mm Tri-X film developed in D-76, diluted 1:1. Nikon FM cameras were used with Nikkor 35mm, 50mm, 105mm and 200mm lenses. My thanks to Marina for making this book a reality.

Cynthia Farah

FOR JIM AND HOWARD

Our gratitude to Carole Barasch, Cathy Jensen, Sil Montoya and to Aria, Barbara, Andy, Elise and Alexa.

Contents

WILLIE NELSON	1	RED STEAGALL	39
MEL TILLIS	3	JOHNNY DUNCAN	41
HOYT AXTON	5	JACKY WARD	43
HANK WILLIAMS, JR.	7	JOHN DENVER	45
DAVID FRIZZELL	9	FREDDY FENDER	47
MICKEY GILLEY	11	LARRY GATLIN	49
JOHNNY LEE	13	FERLIN HUSKY	51
JOHN CONLEE	15	EDDIE RABBITT	53
ERNEST TUBB	17	RONNIE MILSAP	55
RAY PRICE	19	RAZZY BAILEY	57
KRIS KRISTOFFERSON	21	CAL SMITH	59
HANK THOMPSON	23	MARTY ROBBINS	61
KENNY ROGERS	25	WAYLON JENNINGS	63
DON WILLIAMS	27	FREDDY WELLER	65
MOE BANDY	29	GEORGE JONES	67
JOE STAMPLEY	31	GARY STEWART	69
MICHAEL MURPHEY	33	JOHN ANDERSON	71
GENE WATSON	35	MERLE HAGGARD	73
JOHNNY RODRIGUEZ	37	JOHNNY PAYCHECK	75

The fascination with Texas lies in freedom. Wide open spaces. The cowboy image, which is another form of freedom . . .it's very enticing to people living in places like New York City, Chicago or Los Angeles. I was taught since birth, that if you were from Texas, you could do anything you wanted to do because of opportunities. I'd heard those 'bigger and better' Texas brags all my life. I was reluctant to go out in the world and say those things myself because I'd heard 'em so much and I was sick of 'em. But the more places you go and have to compare to Texas, you realize those things aren't bragging statements. They're true.

ON THE ROAD AGAIN • RED HEADED STRANGER • MY HEROES HAVE ALWAYS BEEN COWBOYS • WHISKEY RIVER

Willie Nelson

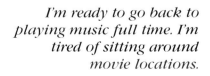

The people who have me depicted as the guy who can do no wrong . . .I know better than that. And the ones who say I'm the most terrible guy in the country . . .I know better than that, too. I lie somewhere in between.

I'm real close with my children, but I'm not much on givin' advice. Just follow me around, watch me and do the opposite, and you'll probably come out okay.

I'm ready to go back to playing music full time. I'm tired of sitting around movie locations.

2

I like acting better than singing. Well, it's a different kind of excitement. I really enjoy it. It takes me back to when I was a child. I used to pretend and play like a lot of things. Acting really takes me back to my youth. Man, I'm playin' house again.

YOUR BODY IS AN OUTLAW • COCA COLA COWBOY • WHAT DID I PROMISE HER LAST NIGHT

Mel Tillis

I've been stuttering all my life and I'm finally beginning to make a helluva living at it.

Things are crazy. Insane. I believe it's gonna get a little worse before it gets better. Here's what we should do. All the countries ought to get together and say, "Okay, we're going back to the beginning." Take all the Jews and put them in Israel. Put all the blacks in Africa. Take Texas, New Mexico and California and give 'em back to Mexico. Take the IRA, the Catholics and Protestants in Ireland...ah hell, take the Irish and find 'em an island somewhere. Just give everything back to all these damn people, start over again and maybe everbody would get their asses straightened out again.

4

My main interest is writing and playing music, but I've also done a lot of TV and film work. I love it. The money's easy. Everybody likes to surround acting with some great mystique. There's nothing to it. You fly in. They pick you up in the limo and take you to your hotel. The limo takes you to location. They comb your hair, put on your clothes, tell you what to say...and pay you well.

BONEY FINGERS • DELLA AND THE DEALER • WILD BULL RIDER • A RUSTY OLD HALO

Hoyt Axton

I did the worst show of my life in Denver several years ago. The next morning I could barely get out of bed. When I looked in the mirror, I couldn't believe it. I looked dead! Right then and there I vowed I'd never look like that again. I haven't touched any cocaine or hard stuff since.

I've got my own label, "Jeremiah Records," named after the bullfrog in my song "Joy to the World." I've been with several record companies and never will be again. They lie to you. Cheat you. They don't pay you. They can't help it though, that's just the way they do business.

Everybody thinks the fall (mountain climbing accident) changed everything. It only delayed my moves by a full two years. Eight operations, a plastic forehead, several scars, partial loss of vision, false teeth and a struggle for survival slowed me down for a while. But before it all happened, I was on my way to finding myself. The doctors brought out that I'd been trained to be, look, sound, sing and act like my father. When they said I was now really like him - almost dead before I reached thirty - I knew they were confirming my own thoughts. Being his son is both a curse and a blessing.

FAMILY TRADITION • TEXAS WOMEN • WHISKEY BENT AND HELL BOUND • OLD HABITS

7

Hank Williams, Jr.

There's nothing I like better than being on top of a mountain, being on the beach or making music that makes people get out of their seats and scream.

A girl from PEOPLE MAGAZINE asked me what I did when I left Music City and moved to Alabama. I told her Charlie Daniels came down. Dickie Betts came down. Marshall Tucker's Toy Caldwell came down. Waylon Jennings came down and we made music. She said, "Darn, those are pretty heavy guys" and I said, "Honey, if you've gone over my musical background, you know that I've done Jim Beam and put sugar in my veins so that makes me a pretty heavy guy."

I've always had a positive attitude about being the brother of someone famous. If anybody's gonna compare me with somebody, it might just as well be with somebody I idolize. That's Lefty Frizzell. He was the greatest.

TEXAS STATE OF MIND • YOU'RE THE REASON GOD MADE OKLAHOMA • LEFTY • LET'S DUET

David Frizzell

Texas people are absolutely one of a kind. It's like home; if you're going home, it means you're going to Texas. I was born in Arkansas, but we grew up in Texas. My dad was in the oil field work and my little brother was born there. We have roots there, and there really is a Texas state of mind.

I think country music has gotten so big because each artist is always trying to better himself and record the best songs. It got really widespread because people like Clint Eastwood, Burt Reynolds and others started using country music for soundtracks in their movies. "Urban Cowboy" helped.

I'm sure the cowboy craze will fade, like everything does. But all that came out of "Urban Cowboy" won't go away. We've been doing it too long here in Texas. Wearin' jeans, boots and hats, dancin' to country music at honky tonks and workin' the chemical plants went on before the movie and will do so long after the film's forgotten.

A HEADACHE TOMORROW • STAND BY ME • DON'T THE GIRLS ALL GET PRETTIER AT CLOSING TIME

Mickey Gilley

I'd love to do an album with Jerry Lee Lewis, and we almost did. But I don't think he'll ever take the time to jack with it. He's the type of guy that when he wants to do something well, he'll do it. And when he does something bad, he's usually bad. I mean, he don't go half way with anything. But he is my cousin and I love him like a brother. He just has some problems.

Most of my time is spent working. For example, we did the Academy of Country Music Awards show. I was off Monday and Tuesday. Wednesday I was in California. I'm here in El Paso tonight. Tomorrow I'll be in Arkansas, in Kentucky Sunday, Monday in Nashville doing "That Nashville Music" and a picture session for a new album that evening. Tuesday, Wednesday and Thursday I'll be recording. Then I'll catch a flight home to Houston, spend one night with my family and head for Dallas. But making music has always been my thing.

When I was bein' raised up on a farm, I always wondered how would I get to travel around the world, sing my songs, have a band, have a good time, meet pretty girls and get paid for it? Zippety-do-da, here I am. I worked hard to get away from that farm; now I'm workin' hard to try and buy one.

LOOKIN' FOR LOVE • ONE IN A MILLION • PICKIN' UP STRANGERS • PRISONER OF HOPE

Johnny Lee

Besides singin', my favorite thing to do is be in love. Just to feel good about bein' with that special woman. To hold her hand. To glow just bein' in her presence. Feelin' happy, content and secure. I haven't been married yet, but I'd like to when the time is right. And have lots of fat little babies.

How long ago could you tune into a country music station and hear Boz Skaggs? They're playing a lot of stuff that didn't have a place before; middle of the road music, which is today's country. Hank Williams, Bob Wills, Ernest Tubb...that's legendary country. The '80s music has just expanded and it'll never die, either.

I just got lucky. Like most everything in life, it's a matter of being in the right place at the right time. I was happy as a D.J. at the radio station and just treated singing as a hobby. If something came of it, I thought it'd be great. If not, I'd still keep fooling with it in my spare time. If my career ever fails, I can always go back to being a farmer or an undertaker.

ROSE COLORED GLASSES • BACK SIDE OF THIRTY • FRIDAY NIGHT BLUES • LADY LAY DOWN

John Conlee

All I want to do now is put out great records. And a great record is one that sells. The reason people fall in love with a song is because it communicates a feeling. The lyrics have to convey an emotion or tell a story people can relate to. That's the commercial value and that's why a person buys a record.

Country music has gotten better and I agree with some of the changes. But they're trying to take it out of the country and western field and I disapprove. Oh, I'll go along with most of it, but you can't make a song jazz or pop or rock and roll and still call it country. A country artist singing with a thirty piece orchestra with clarinets, saxophones and violins isn't playing country music. Well, violins are all right . . .if they're played like fiddles.

LET'S SAY GOODBYE LIKE WE SAID HELLO • WALTZ ACROSS TEXAS • WALKIN' THE FLOOR OVER YOU

Ernest Tubb

Giving up your family is the biggest problem. But if you have it in your system, there ain't much you can do about it. Either you shrivel up and not enjoy yourself, or you can be in the music business.

I wouldn't cut a record tomorrow knowing it would sell ten million copies if I didn't believe in the song.

My music hasn't changed in 40 years. I'm doing the same thing except I have a five-piece band where I used to have only two guitarists. As to my songs, I still want to keep them honest, tell a story that people can identify with and sing with true feeling. That's what country music is all about.

18

What I'm trying to do now is create a marriage of the old style and the new. I hope I'll keep all factions of music lovers happy. I mean, people don't drive 1923 automobiles today. You have to change with the times.

CRAZY ARMS • FOR THE GOOD TIMES • I WON'T MENTION IT AGAIN • HEARTACHES BY THE NUMBER

Ray Price

When I started out in the business, there were only 21 radio stations playing country music. Something had to be done to broaden its appeal, bring it to the city and give it sophistication. I wanted to introduce strings and beautiful orchestration. I was number one then, and I thought I could do this. So in 1967, I hired the Nashville Symphony and recorded "Danny Boy." The song sold a million, but the country disc jockeys thought I deserted our field and they wouldn't play my records. In 1969, I got divorced and moved from Nashville back to Texas. I played some clubs back home, but mostly I prayed for a song that would allow me to do what I wanted musically and gain universal acceptance. My prayers were answered when I received a demo in the mail from a composer named Kris Kristofferson. That song was "For the Good Times" and the rest is history.

Everything is predicated on my writing. Without it, there would be none of the rest. I'm sure they wouldn't have hunted me up in the Gulf of Mexico when I was flying helicopters for a living to come be in a movie. I consider myself a writer first and foremost. The measure of an artist's success, whether in writing, singing or acting, is how you move people.

HELP ME MAKE IT THROUGH THE NIGHT • SUNDAY MORNIN' COMING DOWN • ME AND BOBBY McGEE

Kris Kristofferson

I'm real straight now.
Boring.
Boring as hell.

I've learned to handle celebrity better. I'm not as loose on stage as Willie (Nelson) is, but it's not sheer terror any more. Yea, I'm still scared, and with reason. I've read reviews where they said I acted like I was doing the show with my left hand. Like I didn't care about my performance or my music or my records. And I sweat blood over it! But now I can walk into a crowd of people who might make an ass out of me and it doesn't kill me. I often feel like a public latrine and they're writing on my walls.

One of the greatest pleasures in this business is seeing how many different ways various people can do a song I wrote. Janis Joplin, Roger Miller and Jerry Lee Lewis, just to name three, had completely different versions of "Bobby McGee." I like all of them. I never heard any I didn't like. Even back when nobody paid much attention to me because they didn't know who I was, I was just tickled to get a song cut. You know I went a long time without making any money.

22

Country music has grown from a little bitty business to a gigantic one. The only thing I resent about it is hearing rock music and they're calling it country. Now country's country and rock's rock, but they're playing the same stuff on both country and rock stations. If anybody was a country music fan to begin with, they'd have liked the country music that was already there. They didn't need rock artists, who weren't good enough to fight the competition and make it as a rock star, to come along and say, "Hey, now we're doin' country."

TAKE ME BACK TO TULSA • OLDER THE VIOLIN, THE SWEETER THE MUSIC • KING OF WESTERN SWING

Hank Thompson

When I first started in the business, a honky tonk was something people looked down their noses at. Today it holds a place of distinction. They write books and make movies about 'em.

When country music was distinctly country, all you had to do was hear the intro to the record and you knew who it was. A song would kick off and you knew it was Ernest Tubb, or Bob Wills, Marty Robbins, Hank Thompson. Each was individual. The creative interpretation was there. Now there's been such an homogenization that it all sounds alike. Country music has lost its distinction.

I don't think I have a wonderful voice. But I do have a good ear for the kind of songs I know the public will like.

THE GAMBLER • COWARD OF THE COUNTY • SHE BELIEVES IN ME • LUCILLE

Kenny Rogers

I'm a realist about this business; I've been in it too long. It's like a roller coaster. While I'm at the top, I'm gonna make the most of it because I know it's not going to last very long.

I'm just a regular guy who wants to do a good job. Sometimes I feel like I fall short, but that's probably natural. I want to be honest and sincere with people, as a person and a musician. I'm not big on triangle songs or drinking songs. I wouldn't do one that promoted dope or was anti-religious. "I Believe in You" covers a lot of my beliefs. You have to be true to yourself.

I BELIEVE IN YOU • GOOD OLE BOYS LIKE ME • LAY DOWN BESIDE ME • SOME BROKEN HEARTS NEVER MEND

Don Williams

I think one of the hardest things for people to do, and it has been for me, is to find satisfaction with where they are at any given time. I think we all have a real problem of always looking for the next plane. "Then once I get there, I'll be happy" kind of thought. All of a sudden, you're there and you look around and say, "Hey, I don't feel any different. How come I'm not happy now?" Cause you're looking for that next one. That's a tough nut to crack. I'm not one of the most content people in the world and I have to work real hard at it.

My fondest wish? I guess I'd just like for my kids to find their niche in life and be happy with that. The same for me and my wife. I'm not gonna fight this road the rest of my life. Basically, I just want to be happy.

The first thing everybody wants to do is move to Nashville. I've been in the business for many years and I'd rather live in my hometown, San Antonio, Texas. My family and friends are there. I love to pop in one of the local hangouts and see some of my old buddies, especially the guys I worked with when I was a sheet metal worker. They'll say "Wow, what are you doing here? You're too big for us now." And I'll say, "No I'm not. I've lost a little weight."

CHEATIN' SITUATION • HERE I AM DRUNK AGAIN • SOFT LIGHTS AND HARD COUNTRY MUSIC

Moe Bandy

After busting a bunch of bones and getting pretty bruised up, I quit bull riding. It's safer to sing at the rodeo than it is to ride. It's a way for me to still be part of them without getting killed. My favorite song is still "Bandy the Rodeo Clown," and I sing it for all my cowboy friends.

If I lived my songs, I'd be drinkin' and cheatin' myself to death.

"There's Another Woman" is my life story in a song and it's exactly how I felt when I wrote it. I wasn't trying to offend anybody, I was just sayin' what had happened to me. It's like when Merle Haggard wrote "The Way I Am," about being away fishin'. He wished he was somewhere else besides doin' what he was doin'. That's what country music's all about. Bein' honest. And paintin' a picture of life with the songs.

DO YOU EVER FOOL AROUND • THERE'S ANOTHER WOMAN • IF YOU'VE GOT TEN MINUTES, LET'S FALL IN LOVE

Joe Stampley

The most rewarding thing about this business is bein' my own boss. I worked at a paper mill, a box factory, a soft water service; I was a candy machine vending guy and I've done a little of everything. I was never my own boss 'till the music thing came along. That's what makes me happy: singin' my song and doin' my own thing.

Me and Moe hooked up over a hamburger in London. We got to be pals while we were both singing over there and decided to do some duets together. Shoot, Moe and Joe sounds better than Waylon and Willie.

Country music has changed. Now C and W stations play material they wouldn't have touched before. Country music fascinates me. It's one of the few genres of music which appeals to all ages. I think I'm country rock - with a light element of jazz and a lot of improvisation. Basically, I'm a writer.

WILDFIRE • GERONIMO'S CADILLAC • COSMIC COWBOY • CAROLINA IN THE PINES

Michael Murphey

I lived on a Hopi reservation and I share the basic Indian belief. Life is a circle and man is just part of it. There is no hierarchy. The amoeba is important. You can take life and blow it up to the most incredible intelligence or down to basics. What's important are people and their ideas. Why are we here and where are we going.

Fortunately, I've never messed with drugs in my life. I've never even smoked grass. And I don't drink hardly at all. I've been on stage with 102 degree fever, so sick I couldn't barely hold my head up. You've got to smile and do your show, though. Once you hear the applause, see that you're making the audience feel good and know you're giving them a message with your music, then it's all worth it.

LOVE IN THE HOT AFTERNOON • FAREWELL PARTY • SHOULD I COME HOME OR SHOULD I GO CRAZY

Gene Watson

I do a lot of thinking and worrying...like about the outcome of my songs and what I'll release next. People are critical and they like to pick you apart. I guess I don't feel as secure as a lot of people maybe do. That's probably why I never sold the body tools I work on cars with. You just never know.

I like sad songs. I think 90% of the people are sad nowadays. I don't mean sad, sad all the time, without a smile every once in a while. But I like to reach inside a person and touch that little spot in them. Whether it's a sad song or a happy one, I try to hit that spot and make them know I've been there.

36

I was sentenced to go sing at the veteran's hospital in Tucson. What happened was I had some weed in my suitcase on the airplane. The dogs smelled it, or something like that, at the airport. I had to go to court and the judge sentenced me to sing for the vets on Veteran's Day. It was great. I loved singing for them. Shoot, I felt guilty that I hadn't done it anyway, ya know.

PASS ME BY • RIDING MY THUMB TO MEXICO • WE BELIEVE IN HAPPY ENDINGS

Johnny Rodriquez

I just have to convey the image of myself. Whatever people think of me, I guess that's what I am. No, not sex symbol. That's silly. I just have fun singing and being on stage.

Until 1965, I was in agricultural sales, traveling in the southwest. Since my degree from West Texas State University was in agriculture, that was a logical profession. Then I moved to Hollywood to get my foot in the door of the music industry. Those years were educational and I learned about the business end of the music industry. To learn more from the artist's angle, I moved to Nashville in '72. It didn't really fit my lifestyle. The business attitude was too conservative. The influx of New Yorkers and Californians has made the Nashville people change, but I moved back to Texas in 1976. Texas is the only place I've ever felt at home.

THREE CHORD COUNTRY SONG • HARD HAT DAYS AND HONKY TONK NIGHTS

Red Steagall

Success is not a matter of luck. It's an educated, calculated process: recognize the right kind of song, be with the label that can sell, have the right production and study the business. It doesn't always work out the way you planned, but with ambition and persistence, it'll eventually come together. If you're in a million different places at a million different times, one will turn out to be right.

Even my bad times are good.

My wife ran off with a truck driver. She left me, not holding the bag, but holding three baby girls. We packed up and moved from Nashville back to Texas. While I was tending the farm and bringing up my daughters, the Dolly Partons and the Kenny Rogers of the industry were out working their tails off. Sure, I continued to write and record, but I didn't tour much or make many public appearances. I look up and see that I've had at least 15 Top Ten songs, and people probably know the tunes, but they wonder who the hell Johnny Duncan is.

41   SWEET COUNTRY WOMAN • SLOW DANCING • STRANGER • SHE CAN PUT HER SHOES UNDER MY BED

Johnny Duncan

As to goals, I want to put out good records, win Entertainer of the Year, own thousands of acres of fertile Texas soil, become a respected actor and make one woman happy.

Politically, I'm a conservative. Underneath this long hair is a red neck. I'll speak out on patriotism, religion, the women's movement, anything unrelated to music, and hope I don't offend anyone for spouting off my views. Like if I were to say I loved Anita Bryant and admire her for having the courage to express her convictions, maybe someone who hates her won't buy my records. I feel a person has to be honest. If somebody doesn't agree with me, I hope they'd respect me for having the guts to take a stand and stick to my guns. And, I hope they'll still buy my records, too.

42

All I want is to be accepted by everybody. I think I'm country because country people buy my records and like what I do. I consider myself the new breed of country singer. And I'd like for my music to be accepted internationally.

FOOLS FALL IN LOVE • THAT'S THE WAY A COWBOY ROCKS AND ROLLS • A LOVERS QUESTION

Getting on the bus and leaving home, along with the difficulty of finding the right songs, are the toughest things about this business. But the minute I get on that stage, I don't care about the money, the struggle or the headaches. It all becomes worth it.

I quit drinking. I think I was allergic to the stuff. It made me act funny.

There are a lot of human rights in this country that come out of an incredibly lucky position that don't mean much to a lot of people in the world who are starving to death. There's a crisis going on. The United States has the wherewithal to take a good hard look at the issue and find what role we can take to eliminate hunger on this planet.

𝕿𝖎𝖒𝖆𝖜𝖎 𝕯𝖊𝖓𝖛𝖊𝖗𝖎𝖙𝖊 <u>24</u>

ROCKY MOUNTAIN HIGH • SUNSHINE ON MY SHOULDERS • THANK GOD I'M A COUNTRY BOY

John Denver

I'm an interested person and an active one. I care about the life around me, in whatever form it takes. I've had the opportunity to travel around the world because of my position and I've seen so many great needs. I'd rather spend my time singing. And at concerts, I don't talk about these things. Still, in writing songs, I can communicate much of this. I just can't pass up the opportunity.

*Someday I'd like to quit,
buy some kind of business,
sit down and watch the
dog bark at the car while I
drink a beer.*

YOU'LL LOSE A GOOD THING • BEFORE THE NEXT TEARDROP FALLS • WASTED DAYS AND WASTED NIGHTS

Freddy Fender

You have to change with this world. I felt like I'd been doing the same stuff too long and needed to be more innovative. I'm not getting away from country. I'm just expanding in my own way, putting more Freddy Fender into my music with rock and roll, rhythm and blues and salsa.

Never pass up the opportunity to keep your mouth shut.

I guess I've been called cocky, but I think confident is a better word. When you're a little guy like I am, 5'8", you have to be a little pushy sometimes. I don't want to be a horse's rear, but I feel strongly about things. When you stand up for those things, and prove you're right when other people said you were wrong, they tend to bad mouth you.

ALL THE GOLD IN CALIFORNIA • BROKEN LADY • LOVE IS JUST A GAME • I'VE DONE ENOUGH DYING TODAY

Performing another person's songs or asking somebody to write with you would be like asking somebody to help you make love to your wife. I mean, there are some things you know how to do by yourself.

Larry Gatlin

The controversy over what is and what isn't country was first brought up by some of the traditional artists who were stars. They had their day in the sunshine and all of a sudden their records weren't being played anymore. So a lot of the b.s. is bitterness and sour grapes. Hell, when it's our time to be gone, nobody's gonna have to tell me.

50

Back when I started out, I could count all the guys that was really on records on two hands. There just wasn't that many record labels. And they only had a Top Ten list of songs, where today I guess they've got a Top 100 or maybe Top 500. Country music has gotten so big.

GONE • WINGS OF A DOVE • THERE GOES MY EVERYTHING • DEAR JOHN LETTER

Ferlin Husky

I'm one of the loneliest guys, besides Hank Williams, the world's ever seen. That's why I like to be around people and entertain 'em. Within ten minutes on the stage, after three songs, I've told my life story to the public.

Sure I dig into myself with my music. But if I just wrote for me, I'd probably be the only one listening to my songs. I've got street ideas, a street mind and street pockets. I grew up in a poor family on the streets of New Jersey, and I'm not living up on some hill now so far removed from people and reality that I don't know what's going on. I make music that I hope all people can relate to. That makes 'em feel good and happy.

EVERY WHICH WAY BUT LOOSE • I LOVE A RAINY NIGHT • TWO DOLLARS IN THE JUKEBOX

Eddie Rabbitt

Movies are fine, but as it is, I've turned down 15 scripts. They've had me as a rapist, drug addict, killer, everything. That's not why I got into the music business.

Ask me anything but how to describe myself. I hate that question. I don't know how to answer it. What can I say? I'm 6'1", weigh 195 pounds... and I'm lucky.

As to success, it was more fun working to get there than it is being there.

PURE LOVE • WHAT A DIFFERENCE YOU MADE IN MY LIFE • DAY DREAMS ABOUT NIGHT THINGS

Ronnie Milsap

I've never been bitter about my blindness or considered it a handicap. I talk to a lot of blind kids and try to advise and encourage them. If they have a talent, there's no reason they can't achieve their goals. They just have to push harder.

I love the electricity of a live concert. Recording alone in the studio is okay, but it doesn't come close to the fun and magic of performing for an audience. If that fun level ever drops too low, I'll quit.

56

As a stroke of luck, Dickey Lee recorded "9,999,999 Tears," a song I had written ten years before, and it went to Number One in '76. That got me a recording contract and turned my career around. After trying so many years and seeing things finally start to happen, I felt that I hadn't wasted my life and I wasn't such a dummy after all.

LOVING UP A STORM • YOU'RE A LITTLE TOO OLD TO PLAY COWBOY • ANYWHERE THERE'S A JUKEBOX

Razzy Bailey

I've been talking to a psychic in Florida since 1975. I was depressed at the time, drinking heavily, gaining weight, having legal battles over music, arguing with my wife and my career was going nowhere. My mama suggested I talk to this psychic. She told me things about myself and was accurate. She also told me to keep my chin up and that things were gonna get better. She was right.

I associate music with good times and happiness. I used to listen to my father sing and play the guitar. We lived on a farm in Alabama and it was always fun with everybody getting together, playing instruments, singing and roasting hot dogs. It left a good impression on me. Even at the age of five, I thought it'd be great if I could be an entertainer when I got big. Now I want to go all the way to the top.

I've been on the road for over 20 years. When I first started out, I just felt fortunate to make a living in the music business. If I have good crowds and please the audience, then I'm happy. If I'd gotten into the business for the money, I'd have gotten out a long time ago. Success comes hard and slow. I know what it's like to be poor and not know where the next meal is coming from. I've had lots of money too, and money has caused me mental anguish. With or without money, I still like pork chops and beans. I don't really worry about the future. I've picked cotton, and I don't want to go back to it, but I'm not too good to do it.

COUNTRY BUMPKIN • THE LORD KNOWS I'M DRINKING • SHE TALKED A LOT ABOUT TEXAS

Cal Smith

Three psychics told me I'd go into a slump. They also told me I'd do something bigger and greater than I've ever done.

I was a truck driver, mechanic, laborer and electrician for eight different companies in six months. I stayed on the job just long enough to collect my paycheck. The greatest thing that ever happened to me was discovering I could make a living singing.

EL PASO • WHITE SPORT COAT • ALL AROUND COWBOY • DEVIL WOMAN

Marty Robbins

I justify my actions to myself and to the Man above. If I keep both of us happy, then I'm being a good Christian.

The marquee sign on our bus is always a source of entertainment. I change it frequently; sometimes it says Waylon Jennings, sometimes Loretta Lynn - just whoever I feel like being. Right now the sign reads "Nobody You Ever Heard Of."

I appreciate my family. Them and my music are the most important things in my life...and a few good people around me. I'm just myself...loving my family and doing my own things with my songs. All I want is to try to find peace of mind.

I'VE ALWAYS BEEN CRAZY • DON'T YOU THINK THIS OUTLAW BIT'S DONE GOT OUT OF HAND

It's true I was arrested on cocaine charges. But nothing ever came of it. It was dropped. Drugs are not an important part of my life...Now, do you want to talk about my music or not?

Waylon Jennings

The whole outlaw thing started a long time ago. They said I was a rebel, a renegade, an outlaw. They never understood me. I couldn't conform. I can't. I'm me. You understand what I'm saying? I just didn't do things their way.

I liked country music as a kid, especially Hank Williams as a writer and George Jones as a singer. The lyrics are solid emotion. They make you laugh or cry.

GAMES PEOPLE PLAY • THE PROMISE LAND • BAR WARS • GO FOR THE NIGHT

Freddy Weller

*I don't do much of anything, outside my music, and
I'm proud of it. I don't create things to make myself
interesting or give a good story.*

What you hear on the radio nowadays isn't exactly what I call country music. I sing country music. So does Merle Haggard and Moe Bandy. We don't have too many any more cuz all the good ones went pop. It doesn't bother me at all cuz I'll have the whole field by myself.

HE STOPPED LOVING HER TODAY • ONCE YOU'VE HAD THE BEST • WHITE LIGHTNIN' • BARTENDER'S BLUES

George Jones

Everything I was associated with got me in trouble. Booze. Crooks. Wives. I was so fouled up, I didn't care if I lived or died. But I've got my thinking cap back on now, so all that's water under the bridge.

I'll spend the rest of my life, for what it's worth, making it up to my fans. I've let a lot of people down by not showing up for a show . . .and it wasn't always my fault. A lot of times it was. My fans are so faithful, they've always stood by me.

I'm a man of many moods with my music. I'm boogie woogie. I'm country. I was raised in Kentucky on the music of Chuck Berry, Elvis and Jerry Lee. I've been influenced by the Allman Brothers. Now it's the blues. I don't record to be commercial. Fuck commercialism.

DRINKIN' THING • OUT OF HAND • SHE'S ACTING SINGLE (I'M DRINKIN' DOUBLES) • QUITS

Gary Stewart

We don't play quiet.
We hit you hard with music.
We're all crazy.

My wife understands me and puts up with me. She's a real lady. She knows I love sex, women and drugs.

*I guess you could say I'm like
my music...common and simple.*

SHE JUST STARTED LIKING CHEATIN' SONGS • I'M JUST AN OLD CHUNK OF COAL • YOUR LYING BLUE EYES

John Anderson

My music is very basic...to the point. It's either hard rock and roll or hard country. I'm not middle of the road
Smithsville, Tennessee.

I feel like at least eight different people. My life is always so hectic, I'd like to put everything on hold for a while.

OKIE FROM MUSKOGEE • MISERY AND GIN • MY OWN KIND OF HAT • TODAY I STARTED LOVING YOU AGAIN

Merle Haggard

Today it cost 80 times more to record an album than it used to. The process is so slow, the tracks are laid down months apart and the sound comes out different than when it was recorded. The recording industry has become an electronic game rather than a process of capturing talent on tape.

Yes, I was an ex-con, but that was a totally different person; one I'm not too fond of remembering.

I haven't always been the working man's man. I come from the streets, you understand? They gave me 18 years in prison for 37 counts when I was 17. That's a strong sentence. I'm a true ex-con. So is Merle Haggard. We're the only two. The rest of 'em are bullshit punks. Johnny Cash did one night for two pills. Johnny Rodriguez? Overnight for stealing a goat. Them suckers ain't ex-cons. I'm not proud of being an ex-con and I never want to go back to prison, but I get sick of those punks. Being an ex-con is nothing to brag about. I wouldn't want to do those things again, but I wouldn't change anything, either. I've learned a lot the hard way. Because of everything that's happened to me, I am what I am right now. I'm a red neck, beer drinkin' singer, and always have been.

I'M THE ONLY HELL MY MAMA EVER RAISED • TAKE THIS JOB AND SHOVE IT • ME AND THE IRS

Johnny Paycheck

I'm terribly happy, and that's because I like me and I believe in me. I don't believe in nothin' around me and I don't need nobody. Oh, I need to help people, which I do by my singing. But need 'em? No. I have my musical mistress for companionship. What else is there?

I'm my own man. I've never kissed an ass or licked a boot in my life. I've been wrong many times, but never in my music. My craft is singing and I make a lot of people happy with my songs. I'll probably never have peace of mind, but if I did, I might be a vegetable.

I've been through it all. I've been a junkie, an alcoholic and a pill head. I've lived in penthouses and basements. I've drove Cadillacs and slept under 'em. I've rode freight trains and fought in hobo jungles. I've been in the streets all my life and now I'm a rich man. I have no idea which is better 'cuz it ain't over yet.

FAME AIN'T SHIT.

John Austin Paycheck